Purity is a BATTLE

Purity is a BATTLE

Presented by

BOYFRIEND BEARS

Bold Vision Books
PO Box 2011
Friendswood, Texas 77549

ISBN 9780985356392

Bold Vision Books
PO Box 2011
Friendswood, Texas 77549

Published in association with Books and Such Literary Agency, Santa Rosa, California.
Cover photo by Medcalf Photography, Lynden, Washington.
Cover by Big Fresh, Inc., Bellingham, Washington.
Interior by kae Creative Solutions.
Published in the United States of America.

TABLE OF CONTENTS

ACKNOWLEDGMENTS

Boyfriend Bears is grateful to those who helped bring *Purity is a Battle* to you.

They include our 2012-2013 Boyfriend Bears Teen Board members: Bridget, Daphnee, Holly, Jenah, Kendra, Lauren, and McKenzie; our Executive Board members Kaitlyn Holmgren, Karen Johnson, Stacy Mouat, and Sheila Veldman. We also thank Clark Wiese, husband and dad to Alesha and Madison and by far the biggest supporter of Boyfriend Bears!

Boyfriend Bears is extremely thankful for Stacy Mouat and her passion to provide necessary resources to educate and prepare our youth for the future that God intends for them to have. Stacy compiled and wrote curriculum that focuses on purity, abstinence, consecration, and truth and then granted Boyfriend Bears permission to use the material to help develop a presentation and guidebook for our *Purity is a Battle* curriculum.

Thank you Dannah Gresh and the Pure Freedom Team for the invaluable love and support you showered over Boyfriend Bears during our early years of ministry. We appreciate all of you and the permission to share the Tea Cup Illustration with our *Purity is a Battle* session participants; it's one of our favorites!

We also have the privilege of sharing great illustrations from Passport2Purity. A big thanks to Family Life for their willingness to share these treasures with Boyfriend Bears.

When I look back at how Boyfriend Bears came to be, I remember God's specific calling to missions.

Between the older girls at my school, in my community, and my church it seemed like mission trips were changing many of the lives that influenced me. I wanted to spread the message of Jesus' love and find my purpose when serving Him.

I don't remember being told once that I could change the world...but something inside was telling me different.

After finding an ad in *Sisterhood Magazine*, which links Christian girls from across the globe for a "Never the Same" missions trip to Ecuador I knew I just had to go!

With much prayer and determination, I faced my parents at age 13 to convince them to let me go on this trip to live out my faith. Surprisingly, they said yes, and in a few months time I was on my way to Ecuador!

Each day we would perform an evangelistic drama and would get to tell people about Christ who have never heard about him! Each day of amazing ministry would end with powerful worship and teaching from speakers around the world!

As Dannah Gresh, a national purity author, spoke, I sat moving my feet through the grass in the middle of Quito. My arms flooded with goose bumps as the city air kissed my skin. Without notice, my heart started pumping rapidly; a fire was rising in my soul.

Purity. Living a life full of freedom, making good choices, and being an encouraging role model to the younger set of eyes around me was something I was feeling called to.

At the age of 13, I don't remember once being told that I could change the world at the age I was. It was more along the lines of make a difference, but after high school, college, and adult life…but something inside of me was telling me different. Something told me that with God's help, I could do something about the heartache in the world caused by sexual immorality.

I arrived home with a new glow upon my face and a passion for purity! I started asking myself, "How can I give this fire to others? How can I spread the word about purity, about Jesus' truth and love? How am I going to do this alone?" Thankful, I didn't have to do it alone at all! God is so faithful, and provided answers…almost immediately.

The idea of a stuffed animal bear came to mind. Something that could be hugged and held during the hard times of this journey. It would be my Boyfriend Bear, something to remind me of the passion the Lord had given me and to remember that I am worth the wait!

Purity is a lifestyle, a daily choice, a spiritual motivation to wait! Dannah's message opened my eyes to this truth and ever since then all I've wanted to do is spread the word!

God gave me the vision of Boyfriend Bears, and now they are being used as a tool to open the door to begin conversations about purity all over the United States and beyond!

No matter what your age, you can make a difference! The Lord is just waiting for a prayer of surrender and submission to use your willing heart to further His kingdom! Be lights in this dark world, girls, and glow for the King!

❤ Madison

Purity is a lifestyle, a daily choice, and a spiritual motivation to wait!

NAME

DATE

Boyfriend Bears

Theme Bible Verse

Don't let anyone look down on you

because you are young, but set an example

for the believers in speech, in conduct,

in love, in faith and in purity.

1 Timothy 4:12

We hope that by the end of this session you will have a good understanding of what purity is all about and that you will strive toward God's best for you in the area of sexual purity.

But before we begin, there is something that's really important for you to understand: If you have already had sex or compromised your purity, know that God still loves you.

And He forgives you.

Completely.

Therefore, there is now no condemnation for those who are in Christ Jesus, because through Christ Jesus the law of the Spirit of life set me free from the law of sin and death. Romans 8:1

God heals people (spiritually and emotionally) and leads them into healthy relationships. It's never too late to live a life of purity.

Also, know that if you are a victim of any kind of sexual abuse, it is NOT your fault. And you don't have to walk through it alone. Please find an adult you trust (maybe your mom or youth pastor or a teacher) to help you. Even if it happened in the past, find someone who will listen and help you find resources to help you in the healing process.

There are also hot lines you can call or websites that offer help. For example, Darkness to Light is a national organization that provides information and resources for victims of sexual abuse. Their phone help-line is 1-866-FOR-LIGHT (1-866-367-5444) and the website is www.d21.org.

RAINN (Rape Abuse & Incest National Network) is another national resource. The help-line is 1-800-656-HOPE and the website is www. rainn.org.

LET'S BEGIN THE CONVERSATION

1.   What is **PURITY?**

2.   Why **WAIT?**

3.   How Can Purity Become a
     LIFESTYLE?

(Take a moment to write down your thoughts.)

What does purity mean to me?

_____

_____

_____

_____

_____

_____

_____

_____

_____

_____

1
What is
PURITY?

1

What is PURITY?

❤ The dictionary defines purity as

1) freedom from sin or guilt; innocence; not corrupted by sin

2) freedom from anything that debases, contaminates, pollutes

3) chastity (virginity).

Purity is more than just not having sex.

Jesus defines purity as a heart issue.

Blessed are the pure in heart, for they will see God.

Matthew 5:8

❤ Was I born pure? **YES**   **NO**

Ecclesiastes 7:20

Psalm 51:5

Romans 3:23

❤ So how do I become pure?

_____

_____

He himself bore our sins in his body on the tree, so that we might die to sins and live for righteousness; by his wounds you have been healed. For you were like sheep going astray, but now you have returned to the Shepherd and Overseer of your souls.

1 Peter 2:24-25

If we confess our sins, he is faithful and just and will forgive us our sins and purify us from all unrighteousness.

1 John 1:9

❤ Purity starts in my _____. Then God continues the process of purity in my life. A lifestyle of purity is not always easy or instant. It's something you _____ every day.

As water reflects a face, so a man's heart reflects a man.

Proverbs 27:19

He who began a good work in you
will carry it on to completion until the
day of Christ Jesus.

Philippians 1:6

Therefore, we do not lose heart. Though outwardly we are wasting away,
yet inwardly we are being renewed day by day.

2 Corinthians 4:16

❤ A pure heart leads to pure _____ (thoughts, talk, the way we treat others, sexual purity). What is in my heart/mind will affect what I do. A pure heart helps me make _____ choices.

Romans 12:1-2
Ephesians 4:22-24

❤ I will face _____ in life. They come from desires/_____ within, not from God.

❤ What's lust? It's having an uncontrolled, self-absorbed desire for a person, object, or experience. When I lust, my desire for that person or thing overpowers me.

When tempted, no one should say, "God is tempting me." For God cannot be tempted by evil, nor does he tempt anyone; but each one is tempted when, by his own evil desires, he is dragged away and enticed.

James 1:13-14

❤ It's not a sin to feel tempted. I sin when I dwell on the thought and let it become an action. Saying _____! to lust pushes me toward purity. Whenever wrong thoughts come into my mind, I can pray and ask God to change my thoughts and ways to be like His.

Flee the evil desires of youth, and pursue righteousness, faith, love and peace, along with those who call on the Lord out of a pure heart.

2 Timothy 2:22

No temptation has seized you except what is common to man. And God is faithful; he will not let you be tempted beyond what you can bear. But when you are tempted, he will also provide a way out so that you can stand up under it.

1 Corinthians 10:13

What lusts/desires do I struggle with?

(Circle below or make your own list.)

wanting a boyfriend

obsessing over a crush

wanting attention

wanting the newest stuff

online relationships

wanting the perfect body

worldly affirmation

obsessing over a celebrity crush

wanting to have sex with my boyfriend

popularity

clothes

social media

phone

texting

porn

food

grades

living for myself

_____   _____

_____   _____

*Take delight in the Lord
and He will give you the
desires of your heart.*
Psalm 37:4

2

Why WAIT?

2
Why WAIT?

SPIRITUAL MOTIVATION

Since purity is a heart issue, committing to sexual purity is one way that I can obey God and honor my relationship with Jesus. Moving toward sexual purity strengthens my walk with God.

 Sex outside of marriage is _____God's plan for you.

Flee from sexual immorality...Do you not know that your body is a temple of the Holy Spirit, who is in you, whom you have received from God? You are not your own; you were bought at a price. Therefore honor God with your body.

1 Corinthians 6:18-20

❤ Sexual purity is a _____.

It is God's will that you should be sanctified: that you should avoid sexual immorality; that each of you should learn to control his own body in a way that is holy and honorable.

1 Thessalonians 4:3-4

IS HOLINESS IMPORTANT TO ME?

(Why or why not?)

_____

_____

_____

_____

_____

_____

_____

_____

_____

_____

CHOICES TODAY AFFECT TOMORROW

❤ I won't be a teenager forever. Soon I'll be an adult. God instructs me in His Word to stay _____ for my future husband (and for Him).

Marriage should be honored by all, and the marriage bed kept pure.
Hebrews 13:4

❤ Make good choices today and you'll have no regrets tomorrow.

MAKING THE MOST OF MY TEEN YEARS

❤ Now is the time for me to get to know myself.

HOW DID GOD WIRE ME?

WHAT MAKES ME UNIQUELY ME?

PERSONALITY?

CHARACTER TRAITS?

❤ Now is the time for me to develop my _____ and

discover my _____.

Instead of trying to find the right person, focus on being the right kind of person.

WHAT KIND OF PERSON DO I WANT TO BE?

(Spend time later answering this question.)

_____

_____

_____

_____

_____

_____

_____

_____

_____

EMBRACING THE SINGLE LIFE

❤ See time without a boyfriend (seasons of singleness) as a gift from God—an opportunity to grow, to learn, to serve.

❤ Don't get bogged down in finding or keeping a boyfriend.

❤ Pursue a _____ with God. Find my identity in Christ alone.

It's hard to be happy in a dating relationship if I'm not happy with who I am first.

❤ Allow God to_____ my needs.

He created me and He loves me. He is more interested in me than anyone else. I can commit my heart and emotions to Him and ask Him to keep them safe.

❤ Pursue the dreams and plans God puts in my heart.

DECIDING TO DATE

❤ List reasons that people date:

To have fun

To avoid loneliness

Rebellion

Explore feelings/am I in love?

To find a potential spouse

To be popular

Boredom

To get to know that person

To control/conquer

Friends with benefits

_____

_____

_____

_____

_____

_____

_____

❤ Now circle the reasons that reflect a pure heart.

❤ Spend time listening to the wisdom of parents or respected adults.

Psychologists/counselors agree that young teens are not emotionally ready for serious dating relationships. Think it through/spend time in prayer before deciding to date.

❤ When I am ready, commit to date a guy who is

_____ to Jesus.

Do not be yoked together with unbelievers. For what do righteousness and wickedness have in common? Or what fellowship can light have with darkness?

2 Corinthians 6:14

❤ Check out dating motives. Are they pure or selfish? The guy I date is also a person of worth. Do I want the best for him?

"I have the right to do anything," you say—but not everything is beneficial. "I have the right to do anything"—but not everything is constructive.

1 Corinthians 10:23-24

THE SEASONS OF DISCOVERING TRUE LOVE

💗 _____ SEASON

Begins with attraction; getting to know each other

Spend lots of time exploring personality, compatibility, interests, dreams, and goals. Build the relationship on a _____

_____

💗 _____ SEASON

Exclusive dating, courting, making future plans, proposal

REMEMBER

Words are powerful, and the words,

" _____ "

create a strong emotional bond.

Don't use them flippantly.
Consider saving "I love you" until knowing for
sure he's the one I plan to marry.

Things to Think Through Before
Saying "Yes" When He Pops the Question

- ⊙ Am I sure of his character and integrity?
- ⊙ Are our personalities compatible?
- ⊙ Do our future plans/goals work together?
- ⊙ Does he/will he support God's call on my life?
- ⊙ Do I feel good about his family and their influence on my marriage?
- ⊙ Do we communicate/solve conflict in healthy ways?
- ⊙ Do we have family approval and support?

❤ _____ SEASON

Marriage-as long as we both shall live

WORTH THE WAIT

❤ Marriage isn't just a commitment between a husband and wife. It's a commitment to _____.

It's a _____-a serious forever promise or pledge, not only between husband and wife but also to God.

Malachi 2:14-16

WHEN CHALLENGES COME, ASK GOD FOR HELP AND SOLUTIONS

❤ Marriage is a sacred bond. It is God, not sex, who joins a couple together.

> Then the Lord God made a woman from the rib he had taken out of the man, and he brought her to the man. The man said, "This is now bone of my bones and flesh of my flesh; she shall be called 'woman,' for she was taken out of man." That is why a man leaves his father and mother and is united to his wife, and they become one flesh.
>
> Genesis 2:22-24

Marriage is designed to be the most_____ of all relationships.

❤ Why did God wire me with sexual desires if it's not okay to follow them?

⊙ God created me-and He created sex.

33

- He _____ my sexual nature and desires, but He gave me _____ because He wants the best for me.

- The command to save sex for marriage is for my

   _____.

- It's also for the protection of children. Part of the purpose of sex is procreation (a.k.a. making babies). Healthy marriages offer a better environment for the creation of children who feel loved in the security of family.

CONSEQUENCES OF PREMARITAL SEX

POSSIBLE PHYSICAL EFFECTS

❤ _____

-Each year, almost 750,000 U.S. teen girls become pregnant. (guttmacher.org)

-Of girls who first have sex before age 15, almost half of them will get pregnant. (canyourel8.com)

-Although 15- to 24-year-olds represent only one-quarter of the sexually active population, they account for nearly half (9.1 million) of the 18.9 million new cases of STIs each year. (guttmacher.org)

EMOTIONAL BAGGAGE

-Every teen girl knows that having sex can get her pregnant, but does she know that it can damage her heart?

♥ Premarital sex can lead to _____ of regret, doubt, fear of pregnancy or STIs, fear of rejection, worthlessness/ loss of self-respect, anger at being pressured into having sex, feeling betrayed... (connectioninstitute.com)

♥ 25% of teenage girls who are sexually active report that they are _____ all, most, or a lot of the time (compared to 7% of girls who are not). Studies show that teens (both guys & girls) who are not sexually active are a lot happier than those who are. (heritage.org)

❤ The intimacy of sex impacts a teen's identity development. Chemicals related to bonding increase in a female brain after sex. (Guys don't have this same reaction.) This difference in feelings of emotional bonding can lead to confusion for a girl and can negatively impact her sense of identity. Teens are not emotionally ready for sex. (Dr. Debra Atkisson, child psychiatrist/ parentingwithallthepieces.typepad.com)

❤ Research indicates that casual sex during the teen and young adult years affects the ability to bond later in life. (Hooked: New Science on How Casual Sex is Affecting Our Children by Drs. Joe McIlaney and Freda McKissic Bush)

❤ A study found that women who have sex as young teens are more likely to get divorced. (University of Iowa study; cited in LifeSiteNews.com)

SPIRITUAL EFFECTS

❤ Sex outside of marriage is sin.

❤ Sin robs me of intimacy with God. It _____

my heart and gets in the way of following Jesus with all of my heart,

soul, and mind.

Be imitators of God, therefore, as dearly loved children and live a life of love, just as Christ loved us and gave himself up for us as a fragrant offering and sacrifice to God. But among you there must not be even a hint of sexual immorality, or of any kind of impurity, or of greed, because these are improper for God's holy people.

Ephesians 5:1-3

WHAT SIN IS KEEPING ME FROM A CLOSE RELATIONSHIP WITH GOD?

(Be honest, and write a prayer confessing it to God-remember

He forgives! Ask Him to help you get rid of that sin.)

_____

_____

_____

_____

_____

_____

_____

_____

_____

BENEFITS OF WAITING

❤ Freedom to _____ on my relationship with Jesus
(Psalm 1:1-2)

❤ Joy from obedience (John 15:10-11)

❤ Develops _____

(Galatians 5:22-23)

❤ Confidence from finding my worth in my identity in Christ (John 1:12)

❤ Time to _____friendship

❤ Helps a couple form better communication skills, which lead to a more satisfying, stable relationship (BYU research study, 2010)

❤ Only form of birth control that is _____% effective

DO THE MATH

Everyone is _____ doing it.

❤ 42% of girls/43% of guys in high school have had sex. That means more than half of high school students are virgins.

❤ In a survey of teen guys (ages 15-18), 68% said they "could be happy in a serious relationship that doesn't include sex" and 66% said they would rather "have a girlfriend but NOT have sex." (connectioninstitute.com)

THINK ABOUT IT

I don't _____ anything worthwhile by waiting, but I

_____ a lot if I choose purity.

❤ Doing something for the _____ time creates

strong emotions and feelings that are imprinted on my mind.

Think about a first time you did something big (first day of high school, first time you scored a goal or sang a solo, first time you…). Are you remembering those emotions all over again? You will also remember your first crush, your first love, your first kiss, and your first sexual experience.

❤ There's only one first time for everything.

CHOOSE WELL. CHOOSE PURITY.

3

How Can Purity Become a
LIFESTYLE?

3

How Can Purity Become a LIFESTYLE?

Give my _____ to Jesus. (That's what He wants most of all.)

Outward purity is impossible without inward purity. When I commit my heart to God, the Holy Spirit works in me to make me pure.

Trust in the Lord with all your heart and lean not on your own understanding; in all your ways submit to Him and He will make your paths straight.
Proverbs 3:5-6

❤ Spend time in God's Word.

Like newborn babies, crave pure spiritual milk, so that by it you may grow up in your salvation.

1 Peter 2:2

Sanctify them by the truth; your word is truth.

John 17:17

❤ Spend time in prayer.

Create in me a pure heart, O God, and renew a steadfast spirit within me.

Psalm 51:10

And this is my prayer: that your love may abound more and more in knowledge and depth of insight, so that you may be able to discern what is best and may be pure and blameless for the day of Christ, filled with the fruit of righteousness that comes through Jesus Christ—to the glory and praise of God.

Philippians 1:9-11

UNDERSTAND MY VALUE

I am a person of worth because…

_____ I am made in God's image. (Genesis 1:27)

_____ I am fearfully and wonderfully made. (Psalm 139:13-14)

_____ I am loved. (Romans 5:8)

_____ I am chosen. (1 Peter 2:9)

_____ I am a daughter of the King. (1 John 3:1)

Read these statements again. Place check marks beside the
ones you truly believe. Ask God to help you fully understand
your worth so you can believe all of them.

Tea Cup Illustration…

(What kind of cup do you see yourself as?

Draw a doodle or jot down your thoughts.)

WHEN I FIND MY VALUE IN JESUS I CAN...

❤ Stop playing the _____ _____.

No one ever wins that game. Either I think I'm better than others (resulting in pride or vanity) or I think I'm worse (resulting in self-pity). Either way my focus is on me instead of my Creator.

❤ Say no to _____ _____.

I can be secure in God's approval rather than the approval of the crowd. (Remember, too, that a true friend accepts me and wants me to be my best.)

As iron sharpens iron,
so one person sharpens another.

Proverbs 27:17

❤ Choose _____.

In the way I talk, the way I act and the way I dress.

The dictionary defines modesty as

> 1) freedom from vanity, boastfulness, etc.;
>
> 2) regard for decency of behavior, speech, dress, etc.

The Bible defines modesty as inner holy beauty.

Your beauty should not come from outward adornment, such as braided hair and the wearing of gold jewelry and fine clothes. Instead, it should be that of your inner self, the unfading beauty of a gentle and quiet spirit, which is of great worth in God's sight.

1 Peter 3:3-4

I also want the women to dress modestly, with decency and propriety, adorning themselves, not with elaborate hairstyles or gold or pearls or expensive clothes, but with good deeds, appropriate for women who profess to worship God.

1 Timothy 2:9-10

Clearly women have been thinking about what they wear for quite a long time. Try to choose clothes that reflect inner worth and beauty. The key is to keep the focus on the heart.

SET MEDIA BOUNDARIES

What I watch, read and listen to will influence my thoughts about romance, relationships, and sex. Think it through and use good discernment.

[Pluggedin.com and commonsensemedia.org are good resources for checking out movies, TV shows, books, and music based on positive and negative elements. Each site breaks down content by categories such as sex, language, and violence.]

Finally, brothers and sisters, whatever is true, whatever is noble, whatever is right, whatever is pure, whatever is lovely, whatever is admirable—if anything is excellent or praiseworthy—think about such things.

Philippians 4:8

Spend some time at home thinking and praying about your media diet. Is there anything you need to get rid of to keep your heart and mind healthy?

_____

_____

_____

_____

_____

SET ONLINE BOUNDARIES

Online life and behavior is an important part of my

_____.

Does what I post on social media reflect a heart of purity? Do my online or text conversations with guys reflect a heart of purity?

♥ 21% of teen girls and 39% of teen guys say they have participated in "sexting" with someone they want to date or hook up with. (canyourel8. com)

♥ 51% of teen girls say pressure from a guy is a reason girls send sexy messages or photos/videos. More than 20% of teens say that "pressure from friends" is a reason they send sexually suggestive messages or images. (canyourel8.com)

Use discernment before clicking "send." There's no going back once something is sent electronically. And nothing sent via text/instant messaging or posted online is ever anonymous. Once it's online, it's out there forever.

"Leaky Balloon" Illustration... my take away...

_____

_____

_____

_____

_____

_____

THINK ABOUT IT

When it comes to boundaries, the little things are big.

SET RELATIONSHIP BOUNDARIES

Just like neighbors put up fences to mark and protect property or privacy, people need to set up physical and emotional boundaries in relationships. These boundaries help protect one's heart and values.

Above all else, guard your heart, for everything you do flows from it.
Proverbs 4:23

MAKE A PLAN

♥ It's really important to set _____

boundaries before the kissing begins. It's hard to draw the line once

things get to a certain point.

"Experts in the study of human sexuality have identified seven progressive

stages of physical intimacy:

       1) hand-holding;

       2) arm around the waist;

       3) kissing;

       4) French kissing;

       5) feeling out;

       6) intimate foreplay; and

       7) sexual intercourse.

The important thing to notice is that conscious, willful control tends to

give way to passion after stage #3. After that point, our hormones start

calling the shots." (Focus on the Family)

❤ Law of Progression: Every time I push my limits or go past my boundaries, it gets _____ to go farther the next time and harder to say no.

❤ Set high standards that _____ my value as a daughter of the King.

Many people want to know "How far is too far?" Purity asks a different question: "Does this honor God?"

❤ Choose not what is permissible but what is best.

So I say, walk by the Spirit, and you will not gratify the desires of the flesh.
Galatians 5:16

PRACTICAL TIPS

❤ Spend lots of time with groups of _____ .
(It's healthier and less complicated.)

❤ Start out with group dates. (It's fun, plus there's safety in numbers.)

❤ Don't hang out—go out. Couples get in trouble physically when there's unstructured _____ time.

Besides, a planned, creative date is a lot more fun than watching a movie on the couch!

❤ Play it safe. Avoid the horizontal (even when watching TV) and sitting on laps. Make it off limits to touch anywhere swimsuits and shorts touch.

100% safe = hands off and clothes on

❤ Avoid _____ about physical desires on dates. Words awaken desires.

❤ Say it out loud.

Talk it through with the guy.

Spell out the standards.

If we're not in agreement, it's a red flag.

(Note: If you're not ready to talk about it with him, you're probably not ready to date.)

❤ Get an _____ partner or group.

❤ Choose someone I trust and respect, someone who will ask honest questions and help me stay pure.

❤ Spend time in _____.

❤ Be honest with God. Confess desires and struggles and ask for His help.

BE READY

Steps to Fighting Temptation:

❤ _____ right responses to temptation.

❤ _____ -say "no" and flee if need be

❤ _____ attention; go do something else

❤ _____ my mind; don't let thoughts wander back; start over

KNOW MY RIGHTS

❤ I have the right to be myself.

> I should not be expected to change in order to please someone else.

❤ I have the right to be treated with respect. Always.

> This includes my values, my body, my opinions and thoughts.

❤ I have the right to have friends and activities outside of a dating relationship.

❤ I have the right to say no to sex or any physical act of affection or touch at any time.

> Even if I have had sex before or crossed boundary lines, I have the right to say no.

❤ I have the right to not be pressured or manipulated or made to feel guilty in a relationship.

> True love really will wait.

❤ I have the right to feel safe physically and emotionally.

❤ I have the right to end a relationship that is not healthy.

What NOW?

What NOW?

1. COMMIT TO GOD

We encourage you to make a commitment to God of a life of purity. Ask Him to help you keep your heart, mind, and body pure.

Remember, purity doesn't happen overnight. It is a daily process and a life-long pursuit. You might consider putting your commitment in writing. You can write it yourself or use the Purity Pledge in the back of this book.

PRAY ABOUT YOUR COMMITMENT AND OFFER IT TO GOD AS YOU FILL OUT THE PLEDGE.

2. MAKE LISTS

Think about the kind of woman you want to become. Character? Life goals? How to use your dreams, gifts, or passions to love God and love others? Write it down. Make a "Life List."

REMEMBER, THE KIND OF WOMAN YOU BECOME AFFECTS THE KIND OF WIFE AND MOTHER YOU WILL BE. AIM HIGH!

Think about what you desire in your future husband. Character? Personality? Goals and dreams? Interests and passions? Write it down. Make a "Dream List."

REMEMBER, THIS IS THE KIND OF GUY YOU ARE LOOKING FOR WHEN YOU START DATING. SET HIGH STANDARDS.

3. WRITE A LETTER

Pen your heart-thoughts to your future husband.

We girls on the Teen Board each wrote a letter to our future husband, and we hope you will do the same when you're ready.

Some things we included in our letters were our current interests, a school photo, favorite Bible verses, and promises to him.

Each of us looks forward to sharing the letter with our husband on our wedding day.

4. CHOOSE A SYMBOL

It is helpful to have a visual reminder of your commitment to purity. That's what your stuffed Boyfriend Bear is for. Not only is he cuddly and huggable, he is also that visible symbol of your heart's commitment to God. He even has a secret pocket where you can tuck away your Purity Pledge and your lists and letter. With God's strength and the help of your accountability partners, family—and your Boyfriend Bear—you're ready to pursue a life of purity.

If you have reached this page of *Purity is a Battle,* then you know striving to live a lifestyle of purity will be a hard journey, but it's definitely worth fighting for! You have learned what it means to be pure, to live for God, and to have true joy in your life.

We know from our own personal experiences that temptations will come and that walking this path is not easy. We emphasize this not as a warning but as something to rejoice about. John 16:33 states, "I have told you these things so that in me you will have peace. In this world you will have trouble but take heart! I have overcome the world." As you begin to let God shape you into the woman He wants you to become remember that in your weakness, He is made strong. Go out and show the world the Light where they have not seen it.

We hope that your Boyfriend Bear is as helpful and treasured by you as he is to us. He is a symbol of this journey that you have chosen to embark upon. Keep him in a place where he can remind you of this.

Remember to let God guide you in your daily decisions. Pray to Him continually and live for Him always.

Love and Hugs,
The 2012-2013 Boyfriend Bears Teen Board

Boyfriend Bears
For girls who wait

"I can do all things through Christ who gives me strength"
Philippians 4:13

"From this day on,

I, _____,

pledge before God, in obedience to His Word,
to keep myself pure, to give myself fully,
only to the man that God is
preparing for me.

May this pledge, taken,

_____,

honor You, God, and bring glory to
Your Son, Jesus Christ.
Amen."

_____
Signature

LIFE LIST
Think About The Kind of Woman You Want to Become

My Character _____

_____

_____

My Personality _____

_____

_____

My Goals and Dreams _____

_____

_____

_____

My Interests _____

_____

_____

My Gifts and Passions _____

_____

_____

_____

DREAM LIST
Think About What You Desire in Your Future Husband

His Character _____

_____

_____

His Personality _____

_____

_____

_____

His Goals and Dreams _____

_____

_____

_____

His Interests _____

_____

_____

His Gifts and Passions _____

_____

_____

_____

LETTER TO MY FUTURE HUSBAND

Some things to include: current interests, Bible verses, promises to him, thoughts...

_____

_____

_____

_____

_____

_____

_____

_____

_____

_____

_____

_____

_____

_____

_____

_____

_____

_____

Digging DEEPER

Digging DEEPER

We're so excited that you have participated in the *Purity is a Battle* session. When you're ready we encourage you to dig a little deeper into God's Word:

WHAT?

❤ Spend the next 30 days reflecting (which means the same thing as thinking about) on Scriptures that have been selected from this session guide book.

WHY?

❤ Because God is just waiting to know you better.

HOW?

❤ Begin with prayer. Ask God to guide you as you read and reflect on each Scripture passage.

❤ Look up the Scripture passage in your Bible, read it, and then write it out in the space provided.

❤ Reflect on (think about) God's Word. What might God be saying to you personally? Write it down.

Our prayer is that the next 30 days will transform your heart
and that you will become a bright light in this dark world.

DAY ONE

Begin with Prayer

LOOK UP 2 CORINTHIANS 5:17

Scripture _____

_____

_____

_____

_____

Reflection on God's Word _____

_____

_____

_____

_____

_____

_____

_____

DAY TWO

LOOK UP 1 JOHN 1:9

Scripture _____

_____

_____

_____

_____

Reflection on God's Word _____

_____

_____

_____

_____

_____

DAY THREE

LOOK UP 2 CORINTHIANS 4:16

Scripture _____

_____

_____

_____

_____

Reflection on God's Word _____

_____

_____

_____

_____

_____

_____

_____

DAY FOUR

Begin with Prayer

LOOK UP JAMES 1:13-14

Scripture _____

_____

_____

_____

_____

Reflection on God's Word _____

_____

_____

_____

_____

_____

DAY FIVE

Begin with Prayer

LOOK UP 2 TIMOTHY 2:22

Scripture _____

_____

_____

_____

_____

Reflection on God's Word _____

_____

_____

_____

_____

_____

_____

_____

DAY SIX

Begin with Prayer

LOOK UP PSALM 37:4

Scripture _____

_____

_____

_____

_____

_____

Reflection on God's Word _____

_____

_____

_____

_____

_____

_____

DAY SEVEN

Begin with Prayer

LOOK UP 1 CORINTHIANS 6:18-20

Scripture _____

_____

_____

_____

_____

Reflection on God's Word _____

_____

_____

_____

_____

_____

_____

DAY EIGHT

Begin with Prayer

LOOK UP 1 THESSALONIANS 4:3-4

Scripture _____

_____

_____

_____

_____

Reflection on God's Word _____

_____

_____

_____

_____

DAY NINE

Begin with Prayer

LOOK UP HEBREWS 13:4

Scripture _____

_____

_____

_____

_____

Reflection on God's Word _____

_____

_____

_____

_____

_____

_____

_____

DAY TEN

Begin with Prayer

LOOK UP 2 CORINTHIANS 6:14

Scripture _____

_____

_____

_____

_____

Reflection on God's Word _____

_____

_____

_____

_____

_____

DAY ELEVEN

Begin with Prayer

LOOK UP 1 CORINTHIANS 10:23-24

Scripture _____

_____

_____

_____

_____

Reflection on God's Word _____

_____

_____

_____

_____

_____

_____

DAY TWELVE

Begin with Prayer

LOOK UP GENESIS 2:22-24

Scripture _____

_____

_____

_____

_____

_____

Reflection on God's Word _____

_____

_____

_____

_____

_____

_____

DAY THIRTEEN

Begin with Prayer

LOOK UP EPHESIANS 5:1-3

Scripture _____

_____

_____

_____

_____

Reflection on God's Word _____

_____

_____

_____

_____

_____

_____

DAY FOURTEEN

Begin with Prayer

LOOK UP PSALM 1:1-2

Scripture _____

_____

_____

_____

_____

_____

Reflection on God's Word _____

_____

_____

_____

_____

_____

DAY FIFTEEN

Begin with Prayer

LOOK UP JOHN 15:10-11

Scripture _____

_____

_____

_____

_____

Reflection on God's Word _____

_____

_____

_____

_____

_____

_____

DAY SIXTEEN

Begin with Prayer

LOOK UP GALATIANS 5:22-23

Scripture _____

_____

_____

_____

_____

Reflection on God's Word _____

_____

_____

_____

_____

_____

DAY SEVENTEEN

Begin with Prayer

LOOK UP PROVERBS 3:5-6

Scripture _____

_____

_____

_____

_____

Reflection on God's Word _____

_____

_____

_____

_____

_____

_____

DAY EIGHTEEN

Begin with Prayer

LOOK UP 1 PETER 2:2

Scripture _____

_____

_____

_____

_____

Reflection on God's Word _____

_____

_____

_____

_____

DAY NINETEEN

Begin with Prayer

LOOK UP PSALM 51:10

Scripture _____

_____

_____

_____

_____

Reflection on God's Word _____

_____

_____

_____

_____

_____

_____

DAY TWENTY

Begin with Prayer

LOOK UP PHILIPPIANS 1:9-11

Scripture _____

_____

_____

_____

_____

_____

Reflection on God's Word _____

_____

_____

_____

_____

_____

DAY TWENTY-ONE

Begin with Prayer

LOOK UP GENESIS 1:27

Scripture _____

_____

_____

_____

_____

Reflection on God's Word _____

_____

_____

_____

_____

_____

_____

DAY TWENTY-TWO

Begin with Prayer

LOOK UP PSALM 139:13-14

Scripture _____

_____

_____

_____

_____

_____

_____

Reflection on God's Word _____

_____

_____

_____

_____

_____

_____

DAY TWENTY-THREE

Begin with Prayer

LOOK UP ROMANS 5:8

Scripture _____

_____

_____

_____

_____

_____

Reflection on God's Word _____

_____

_____

_____

_____

_____

_____

DAY TWENTY-FOUR

Begin with Prayer

LOOK UP 1 PETER 2:9

Scripture _____

_____

_____

_____

_____

Reflection on God's Word _____

_____

_____

_____

_____

_____

DAY TWENTY-FIVE

Begin with Prayer

LOOK UP 1 JOHN 3:1

Scripture _____

_____

_____

_____

_____

Reflection on God's Word _____

_____

_____

_____

_____

_____

_____

_____

DAY TWENTY-SIX

Begin with Prayer

LOOK UP 1 PETER 3:3-4

Scripture _____

_____

_____

_____

_____

_____

Reflection on God's Word _____

_____

_____

_____

_____

_____

_____

DAY TWENTY-SEVEN

Begin with Prayer

LOOK UP PHILIPPIANS 4:8

Scripture _____

_____

_____

_____

_____

Reflection on God's Word _____

_____

_____

_____

_____

_____

_____

DAY TWENTY-EIGHT

Begin with Prayer

LOOK UP PROVERBS 4:23

Scripture _____

_____

_____

_____

_____

Reflection on God's Word _____

_____

_____

_____

_____

DAY TWENTY-NINE

Begin with Prayer

LOOK UP GALATIANS 5:16

Scripture _____

_____

_____

_____

_____

_____

Reflection on God's Word _____

_____

_____

_____

_____

_____

_____

DAY THIRTY

LOOK UP 1 TIMOTHY 4:12

Scripture _____

_____

_____

_____

_____

_____

_____

Reflection on God's Word _____

_____

_____

_____

_____

_____

_____

ANSWER KEY

1. WHAT IS PURITY?

Page 19	commit my heart to Jesus, heart, pursue
Page 20	choices, right, temptations, lusts
Page 21	No

2. WHY WAIT?

Page 24	never
Page 25	choice
Page 26	pure
Page 27	interests, passions
Page 28	relationship, meet
Page 30	committed
Page 31	consideration, foundation of friendship, commitment, "I Love You"
Page 32	cementing, God, covenant
Page 33	intimate
Page 34	designed, boundaries, protection, Pregnancy
Page 35	Sexually Transmitted Infections, feelings, depressed
Page 37	entangles
Page 38	focus, self-control
Page 39	enjoy, 100%, not
Page 40	lose, gain, first

3. HOW CAN PURITY BECOME A LIFESTYLE?

Page 42	heart
Page 45	comparison game, peer pressure, modesty
Page 48	reputation
Page 50	physical
Page 51	easier, reflect, friends
Page 52	alone, talking
Page 53	accountability, prayer, rehearse, resist, redirect, renew

ABOUT US

Hey girls (and moms!),

We are a daughter-mother team serving in a ministry that is definitely inspired by God!

As a daughter, I'm so thankful for the opportunity to spend time with my mom working for the Kingdom and learning something new about Jesus every day. There's nothing cooler than learning about God from my mom and being able to bless other girls with this ministry!

As a mother, there is nothing more joyful than being where God wants me to be and being able to teach girls about purity and the choices that are available to them. Growing up, I didn't understand that I made choices which have led to many consequences that still affect me today. Through this ministry, God has showered me with His amazing grace and has renewed my heart!

We can't imagine how our lives would be today without being involved in this ministry or experiencing God's grace and faithfulness. If Boyfriend Bears has taught us anything, it's that God uses the least, the ordinary, and the unequipped.

We live in Lynden, WA, along with an amazing father/husband, Clark, and one awesome brother/son Cam. And we can't forget our sweet Wheaten Terrier, Ozzy!

 *Madison and Alesha*

We'd love to hear from you!

Send us a note to tell us about your session experience or let us know how we can encourage you or pray for you.

www.BoyfriendBears.org

or

Boyfriend Bears

P.O. Box 375

Lynden, WA 98264